WORSE
THAN DAD JOKES

Tarphy W. Horn

Also by Tarphy W. Horn

Trapped Inside the Maelstrom: Tales of Horror and Madness

Darkness In Aspen Grove

To my friends and family, who've listened to my constant puns and jokes for many, many years.

www.tarphywhorn.com

ISBN 978-1-7373698-2-0

Many of the proverbs and adages used in this book have been around for hundreds of years. They have all sorts of origins: famous novels, the writings of theologians, the words of politicians, old wives' tales, and so on. Some of these pearls of wisdom originated as far back as the fourteenth century and barely even make sense in today's society. Those, of course, make the best joke fodder.

If you enjoy limerick style humor, sarcasm, and puns, this book was written for you.

I feel compelled to point out that nothing in this book should be taken as actual advice. Enjoy responsibly. For best results, read out loud.

T. W. H.

WORSE THAN DAD JOKES

1. *Curiosity killed the cat.*
Curiosity is still at large; if sighted, approach with extreme
caution.

$\approx \circ \ll$

2. *Let sleeping dogs lie.*
Then wake them up and make them confess the truth. Demand
answers. Somebody chewed up the toilet paper, and the cat has
an alibi.

$\approx \circ \ll$

3. *Don't count your chickens before they hatch.*
After they hatch, they'll be running around, and you won't be
able to count them then, either. You should probably just
forget about the chickens.

4. *Better late than never.*
Unless you need CPR.

❧❧

5. *If you can't stand the heat, get out of the kitchen.*
Don't go in the bedroom, either.

❧❧

6. *Honesty is the best policy.*
Unless you're about to die. Then life insurance is the best
policy.

❧❧

7. *Time flies when you're having fun.*
Otherwise, it walks.

8. *You don't always get what you want.*
Sometimes you get what your cat wants. Whatever you decide
to do with that catnip stays between you and your bong.

9. *Necessity is the mother of invention.*
No one knows who the father is.

10. *An apple a day keeps the doctor away.*
So does being broke.

11. *Two heads are better than one.*
Unless you share a neck.

12. *Never put off until tomorrow what can be done today.*
Then tomorrow you can put off what could've been done until
the next day, and you can get a day off.

※

13. *Give a man a fish, he eats for a day. Teach a man to fish,*
he eats for a lifetime.
Teach a fish to stay away from man, and the fish will live a lot
longer.

※

14. *The road to Hell is paved with good intentions.*
Concrete was too expensive.

15. *You can't judge a book by its cover.*
Even if the cover is a criminal, the book may have done
nothing wrong.

ॐॐ

16. *In one ear, out the other.*
Or, in medical terms, in one ear, through the auditory canal,
into the Eustachian tube, down the throat, into the stomach,
through the small intestine, through the large intestine, and out
the other–Wait! That's not the other *ear*!

ॐॐ

17. *Good things come to those who wait.*
Good fish come to those with bait.

18. *What goes up must come down.*
Unless it splatters across the underside of an airplane. Then it's definitely staying up, at least until the plane lands.

19. *Speak of the devil and he will appear.*
It's easier than using a summoning ritual, and no animal sacrifice is required.

20. *We'll cross that bridge when we come to it.*
Unless there's a troll. Then we'll have to swim under the bridge, cause no troll is taking our gold.

21. *You can't teach an old dog new tricks.*
You can't teach him about Schrodinger's cat, either. Or can you?

❧

22. *Everything's going to hell in a handbasket.*
As the handbasket gets closer to hell, it grows hotter and hotter. Then it melts, and everything has to walk the rest of the way to hell.

❧

23. *Even a broken clock is right twice a day.*
Unless it's married.

24. *What's good for the goose is good for the gander.*
Unless the goose is in a pan in the oven set at 350 degrees.

&ersed;

25. *Don't get caught red-handed.*
Wear gloves so no one knows what color your hands are.

&ersed;

26. *Don't jump the gun.*
Walk around it.

&ersed;

27. *Don't cut off your nose to spite your face.*
Your nose ring will thank you; it doesn't want to be homeless.
Neither do your boogers.

28. *You get what you pay for.*
If you're a thief, you get what you don't pay for.

৯৽৽৻ঌ

29. *Children should be seen and not heard.*
Or tripped over. Or stepped on.

৯৽৽৻ঌ

30. *When in Rome, do as the Romans do.*
Or don't. Build an igloo. Confuse the fuck out of the Romans.

৯৽৽৻ঌ

31. *The pen is mightier than the sword.*
But don't bring a pen to a sword fight.

32. *Lie down with dogs, and you'll wake up with fleas.*
Lie down with fleas, and you'll wake up itchy.

꙾

33. *History repeats itself.*
Itself. Itself. Itself.

꙾

34. *Cleanliness is next to godliness.*
Filthiness can't be next to godliness until cleanliness stops being rude and gets out of the way.

꙾

35. *One man's trash is another man's treasure.*
So don't go deep sea diving. Go dumpster diving.

36. *A picture is worth a thousand words.*
An English dictionary is worth $19.99, and it has 829,000 words.

❧❧

37. *Haste makes waste.*
Haste will also get you a speeding ticket, and getting pulled over wastes even more time.

❧❧

38. *Don't talk the talk if you can't walk the walk.*
Especially if you have trouble doing two things at once.

❧❧

39. *The apple doesn't fall far from the tree.*
It may bounce, however, and roll down a hill, so where it lands is anybody's guess.

40. *Two's company; three's a crowd.*
Four's a city, and you can incorporate.

ಶ್ಠಿ

41. *If it isn't broken, don't fix it.*
If it is broken, return it to the store and get your money back.

ಶ್ಠಿ

42. *Measure twice, cut once.*
Swear as many times as necessary.

ಶ್ಠಿ

43. *Loose lips sink ships.*
   Loose lips can also fall right off your face, so be careful.

44. *There's no place like home.*
Thank God.

⚜

45. *People who live in glass houses shouldn't throw stones.*
They should buy curtains.

⚜

46. *Early to bed and early to rise, makes one healthy, wealthy, and wise.*
But sleeping late helps you recover from your hangover.

⚜

47. *Put your money where your mouth is.*
Eat a bank.

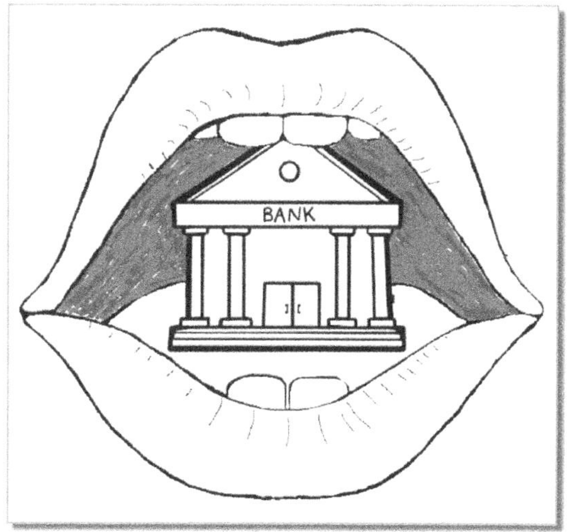

48. *Silence is golden.*
Noise is purple.

჻

49. *Rome wasn't built in a day.*
The Ancient Romans must've been slackers.

჻

50. *A bird in the hand is worth two in the bush.*
But birds in the bush can't bite you. They can only stare.

჻

51. *Money doesn't grow on trees.*
Well, actually, money is made of paper. Paper is made from wood. Wood comes from trees.

52. *Too many cooks spoil the broth.*
The broth is already a spoiled brat, yet they keep buying it fancy new ladles and bowls.

53. *The best way to a man's heart is through his stomach.*
You shouldn't try to get to it without a surgeon, however.

54. *A penny saved is a penny earned.*
It's also a penny taken out of circulation, resulting in a decrease in the money supply, contributing to interest rates rising, making it cost more to borrow money to buy a truck.

55. *Don't let the cat out of the bag.*
It's a waste of time. The cat will just crawl right back inside.

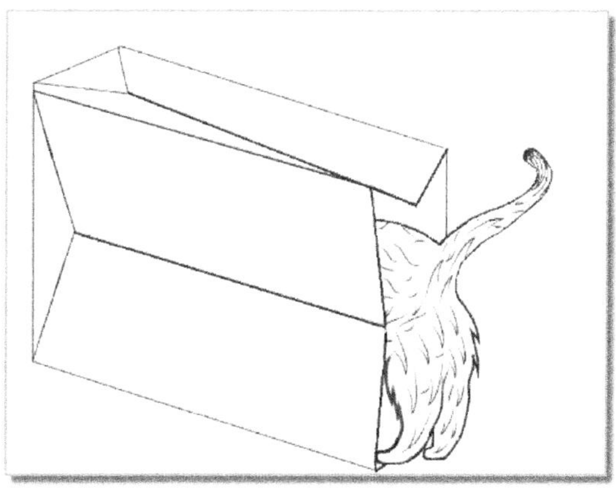

56. *If you snooze, you lose.*
But at least you'll be well-rested.

❧

57. *Great minds think alike.*
That's why we have patents and copyrights.

❧

58. *Do unto others as you would have done to you.*
Unless you're a masochist.

❧

59. *A stitch in time saves nine.*
Nine lives. By repairing your clothing, you are saving a cat.

❧

60. *Don't judge a person until you've walked a mile in their shoes.*
Then you can judge their shoes, too.

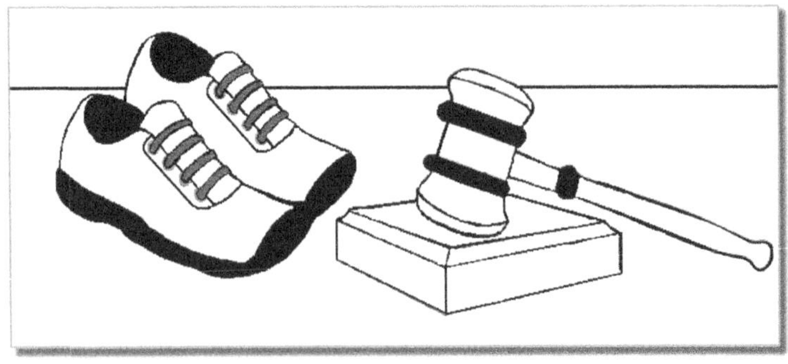

61. *Don't beat around the bush.*
Don't beat under the bush, either. You'll run into the roots and kill the bush.

⊱⋅⊰

62. *Sometimes, life hands you a lemon.*
But it's more likely to hand you an onion, so when it does, take that thing, slice it up, and eat it on a grilled hamburger with barbecue sauce and pickles.

⊱⋅⊰

63. *When the cat's away, the mice will play.*
They'll play violins. They're musically gifted.

⊱⋅⊰

64. *Keep a sharp eye out.*
If you keep it in, it will poke your brain.

65. *You can't make an omelet without breaking a few eggs.*
You also have to peel an onion, melt some cheese, and chop up some peppers. Cooking is violent.

66. *It takes two to tango.*
It only takes one to pole dance. Pole dancing is more efficient.

67. *Bite your tongue.*
Just don't bite too hard, or it'll bleed for at least a day and a half. And stitches taste awful.

68. *Don't look a gift horse in the mouth.*
Look it in the eye. Stare it down. Assert your dominance.

69. *Life imitates art.*
Art gets tired of life mocking it, so art sticks its tongue out at life. They both act like children.

જ઼ન

70. *When one door closes, another door opens.*
Hopefully, it's the patio door. Then the dog can finally get back in the house. He's getting lonely outside. And cold.

જ઼ન

71. *Sticks and stones may break your bones, but words will never hurt you.*
Unless the words are in a really heavy dictionary that falls on your head.

72. *Better safe than sorry.*
It's better not to break into someone's safe, or you're likely to be sorry. Especially if you get arrested.

⤞⤝

73. *Expect the unexpected.*
But don't let on that you expected your surprise party. Your friends worked hard to blow up all those balloons. They spent a lot of money on you. They would never throw a surprise party for you again.

⤞⤝

74. *Money is the root of all evil.*
Spend it quickly before it starts growing demons.

75. *There's no time like the present.*
There's no present like a million bucks.

76. *Don't put all your eggs in one basket.*
Hide them. Make the Easter Bunny work to find them for a change.

77. *Hindsight is 20/20.*
Foresight is a dollar and a half.

78. *Don't let one bad apple spoil the whole bunch.*
Take the bunch and make a pie, and hurry!

79. *All's well that ends well.*
And if no one ends up in a well, that's a bonus.

੭ৢৼৢ৾

80. *All that glitters isn't gold.*
Sometimes it's purple, like noise.

੭ৢৼৢ৾

81. *Hell hath no fury like a woman scorned.*
Hell hath been trying to produce more of this kind of fury for mass distribution without using a woman scorned, but so far, they haven't been successful.

੭ৢৼৢ৾

82. *Third time's a charm.*
By the tenth time you'll have a whole charm bracelet.

83. *Look before you leap.*
Leap before the train hits you.

84. *Don't beat a dead horse.*
It can't fight back, and that's not fair.

85. *A journey of 1,000 miles starts with a single step.*
And a call to the bank to borrow money.

86. *Knowledge is power.*
Having an idea is a power surge.

87. *He who dies with the most toys wins.*
And he better have one hell of a lot of batteries and a screwdriver.

❧

88. *You catch more flies with honey than with vinegar.*
Fly paper also works.

❧

89. *It's not over till it's over.*
Then it goes under and starts all over. It's an endless cycle. It will *never* be over.

❧

90. *Don't make a mountain out of a molehill.*
Make a tourist attraction. Charge people to see it.

91. *There's no such thing as a free lunch.*
If someone gives you a sandwich and chips, it will destroy spacetime.

⊷

92. *You don't know what you've got until it's gone.*
Technically, you don't know what you've got until you take inventory.

⊷

93. *If you're not part of the solution, you're part of the problem.*
Always be the a^2. Never be the $b^2 + c^2 - bc(\cos)A$.

⊷

94. *The early bird catches the worm.*
The worm should have slept in.

95. *Actions speak louder than words.*
Better yet, actions can't be misspelled or pronounced
incorrectly.

ఈం•ఴ

96. *You can't have your cake and eat it too.*
So throw it on the ground and step on it so no one else can eat
it either. Be bitter about sweets from now on.

ఈం•ఴ

97. *If you break a mirror, you'll have seven years of bad luck.*
Worse than that, you'll have a broken mirror. You'll probably
cut yourself cleaning up the mess.

ఈం•ఴ

98. *The squeaky wheel gets the grease.*
It puts the grease in a deep fat fryer and makes donuts.
Uneaten donuts, of course, grow up to be wheels.

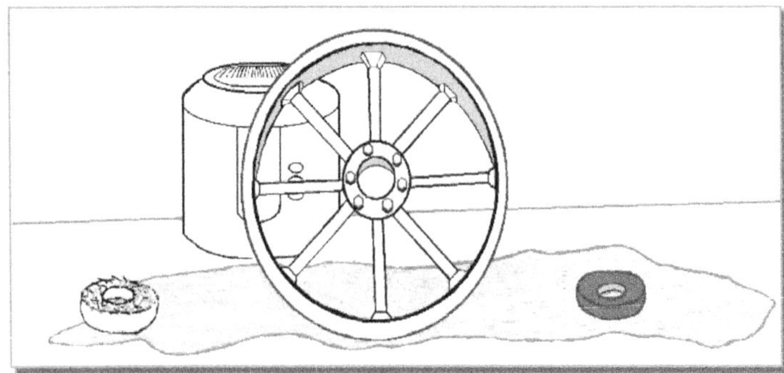

99. *You can lead a horse to water, but you can't make him drink.*
He's as stubborn as a mule. He's also passive-aggressive. He hasn't forgiven you for the cart.

100. *There's more than one way to skin a cat.*
But if you come for the cat, the crazy cat ladies will beat your ass. And rightfully so. The cat doesn't deserve to be punished.

101. *The writing's on the wall.*
It's telling the spiders to go back to the corners of abandoned buildings where they belong. This has proven ineffective in getting them to leave, however, since spiders are unable to read.

102. *It's no use crying over spilled milk.*
The tears will just add to the puddle, and you'll have a bigger
mess to clean up.

❧

103. *No pain, no gain.*
No gain, no pain.

❧

104. *A rolling stone gathers no moss.*
Probably because it doesn't have hands to gather moss with.
Don't judge. It's not the stone's fault.

❧

105. *The grass is always greener on the other side of the hill.*
This creates a paradox where the value of green becomes
infinite.

106. *All work and no play makes Jack a dull boy.*
It also forces him to deal with his boss all day.

⁂

107. *Familiarity breeds contempt.*
So don't get familiar with anyone. Breed something useful,
like fluffy chickens.

⁂

108. *A chain is only as strong as its weakest link.*
Someone needs to make the weakest link lift weights so it gets
stronger.

⁂

109. *All is fair in love and war.*
Some affairs have led to war.

⁂

110. *The devil's in the details.*
Someone needs to get him out of there before he gets all the
details messed up.

111. *If you don't have anything nice to say, don't say anything at all.*
Seethe in silence.

112. *A fool and his money are soon parted.*
Especially if the fool drops his wallet.

113. *No man is an island.*
The people who named the Isle of Man were liars.

114. *Lightning never strikes the same place twice.*
People would be shocked if it did.

115. *A watched pot never boils.*
The liquid in the pot does, though.

116. *Two wrongs don't make a right.*
They make you even more lost. You might want to get out your GPS.

117. *Where there's smoke, there's fire.*
There's also a wide variety of chemicals that are bad for you. Be like Bill Clinton and don't inhale.

118. *Seeing is believing.*
Closing your eyes is disbelieving.

119. *If you want something done right, do it yourself.*
If you want something done left, do it backwards.

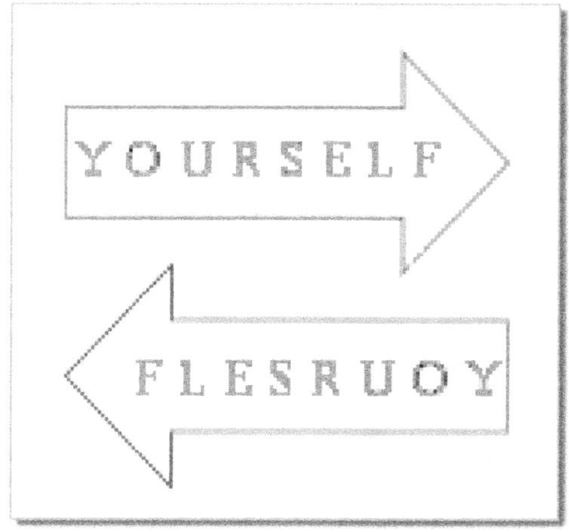

120. *If at first you don't succeed, try, try again.*
If you still don't succeed, consider it a sign, and do something else.

❧

121. *Don't bite the hand that feeds you.*
Especially if you're a zombie. The last thing this world needs right now is more zombies.

❧

122. *It's easier said than done.*
So let's kick back, have some wine, and gossip about someone else doing It.

❧

123. *Beauty is in the eye of the beholder.*
Better give the beholder some eye drops. That's gotta hurt.

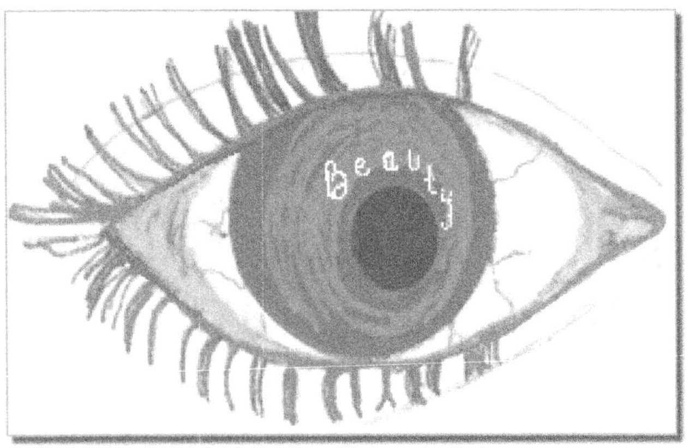

124. *Better the devil you know than the one you don't.*
The devil you know might be fake. When the time comes to begin eternal torture, you want the real thing, not some cheap substitute.

೫೪

125. *Birds of a feather flock together.*
They do other things together, too. Secret things.

೫೪

126. *When the going gets tough, the tough get going.*
To the liquor store.

೫೪

127. *Keep your friends close and your enemies closer.*
Keep your cat closest of all, because she's soft.

128. *Blood is thicker than water.*
Unless you're taking blood thinners.

128. *Blood is thicker than water.*

129. *Ignorance is bliss.*
Just look at all the happy politicians.

130. *Waste not, want not.*
No one wants waste.

131. *A leopard can't change its spots.*
A zebra can't change its stripes.
Chameleons are lucky.

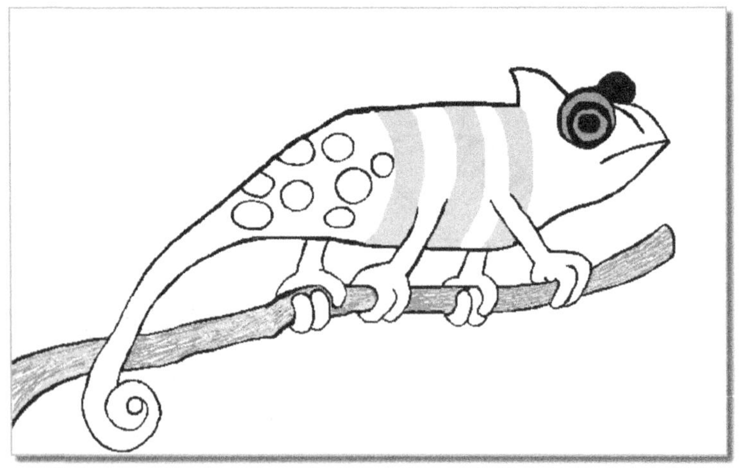

132. *Still waters run deep.*
Flowing waters run fast. Drinking water runs through the body. Who knew water was so athletic?

⬥

133. *A man's home is his castle.*
A woman's home is her kingdom.

⬥

134. *No news is good news.*
Good news is rare. Bad news is everywhere. Fuck news.

⬥

135. *An eye for an eye, a tooth for a tooth.*
It's cheaper than trading kidneys, and no one ends up in a bathtub full of ice.

⬥

136. *Kill two birds with one stone.*
Or get two birds stoned, and nobody has to die.

137. *Shit rolls downhill.*
Said no astronaut ever.

∂∽∾

138. *Cold hands, warm heart.*
Cold feet. Hot-blooded. The human body is clearly confused by temperature.

∂∽∾

139. *Beauty is only skin deep.*
Your internal organs are ugly.

∂∽∾

140. *Money talks.*
But it rarely says anything of interest.

∂∽∾

141. *Laughter is the best medicine.*
Sorry, penicillin.

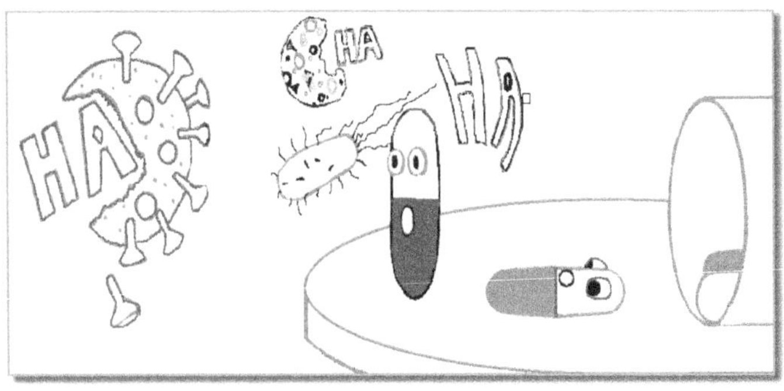

142. *Hope for the best, but prepare for the worst.*
The *brat*wurst. It could show up at any time. Be ready. Go buy sourcrout and onions.

143. *Absence makes the heart grow fonder.*
But it doesn't make your ex any hotter.

144. *The ends justify the means.*
Even if, by the end, you've become mean.

145. *Don't go off half-cocked.*
Take the entire rooster.

146. *Revenge is a dish best served cold.*
If it's served hot, they might enjoy it. Make sure to cover it with salt, and maybe some laxatives.

⊰•⊱

147. *Fool me once, shame on you. Fool me twice, shame on me.*
Fool me three times, and you are *seriously* in need of a new hobby.

⊰•⊱

148. *Every dog has its day.*
Every cat has every day.

149. *Don't sugarcoat it.*
If it tastes too good, they'll expect you to bake it again.

愉愉

150. **Fortune** *favors the bold.*
Misfortune favors italics.

愉愉

151. *In for a penny, in for a pound.*
In for a cent, in for a centigram.

愉愉

152. *You only get out of something what you put into it.*
This becomes apparent when you eat jalapeño peppers.

153. *A friend in need is a friend indeed.*
And is probably a friend in deep shit.

જ⚬ઙ

154. *Out of sight, out of mind.*
Out of skull. Out of body. Out of reality.

જ⚬ઙ

155. *To each his own.*
Don't share. Go ahead and be selfish. Keep your own to
yourself.

જ⚬ઙ

156. *You reap what you sew.*
It's a pretty grim prospect for your torn clothes.

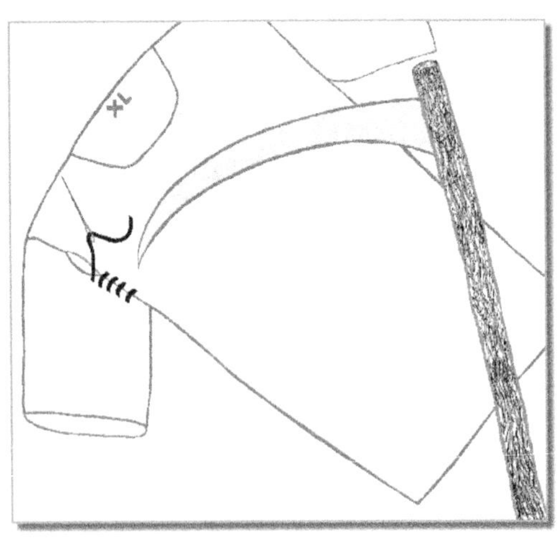

157. *Where there's a will, there's a way.*
Where there's a way to get into the will, go for it.

158. *You've made your bed. Now you have to lie in it.*
Or jump on it. Or have a pillow fight.

159. *Once bitten, twice shy.*
Thrice bitten, and if you're not a vampire by now, you must be immune to vampirism.

160. *Forewarned is forearmed.*
Four-armed is half an octopus.

161. *If you can't beat 'em, join 'em.*
This applies specifically to young children.

❧⚜❧

162. *Busy hands are happy hands.*
Idle hands are exhausted from being busy hands.

❧⚜❧

163. *It's a dog-eat-dog world.*
Dog food must taste awful if it has turned dogs into cannibals.

❧⚜❧

164. *Easy come, easy go.*
The exception to this is constipation. There's nothing easy about going when you're constipated.

❧⚜❧

165. *Time is money.*
Money is also money.

166. *Be careful what you wish for.*
Make sure you speak clearly so you don't end up with a mummy instead of money.

❧

167. *Don't throw out the baby with the bath water.*
You'll get arrested.

❧

168. *A house divided cannot stand.*
A house with a broken foundation can't stand, either.

❧

169. *There's safety in numbers.*
There's only danger in letters.

170. *If wishes were horses, beggars would ride.*
If horses had wishes, riders would beg.

❦❧

171. *What goes around, comes around.*
Try this. Pass out hundred-dollar bills. See if anyone gives them back.

❦❧

172. *A mind is a terrible thing to waste.*
So when you're done with it, recycle; let the worms eat it.

❦❧

173. *Home is where the heart is.*
You no longer need a rib cage.

174. *Don't put the cart before the horse.*
The horse will trip, causing the cart to tip over and break into pieces. The horse will be pissed. He was already having a bad day.

⮞⮜

175. *Misery loves company.*
And companies thrive on misery.

⮞⮜

176. *Laugh and the whole world laughs with you. Cry and you cry alone.*
Laugh until you cry, and it confuses everybody.

⮞⮜

177. *Every cloud has a silver lining.*
It's amazing no one has figured out how to mine that silver yet.

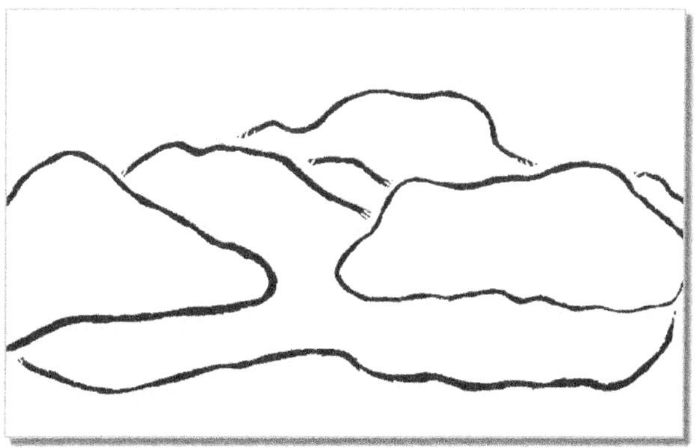

178. *When it rains, it pours.*
Sometimes it floods. Buy a boat just in case.

☙❧

179. *Time waits for no one.*
It's impatient and selfish.

☙❧

180. *Slow and steady wins the race.*
If you're racing turtles. Or snails.

☙❧

181. *What goes around, comes around.*
Then it gets dizzy and falls over.

☙❧

182. *All good things must come to an end.*
Including this book.

Made in the USA
Monee, IL
07 July 2026

56553282R00038